WISH UPON A SNOWFLAKE

By

Tiago Hartel Das Fontes

About The Author

An unrealised artist, an admirer of Michael Morpurgo, and avid reader, Tiago Hartel Das Fontes is a regular student with ambitions to become a renowned journalist.

Born in London, lives now rurally with his parents and a little brother.

Tiago wants to travel the world with a desire to walk in the wilderness, discover new cultures and cuisines. He loves to read not only books but also geographic and animal magazines.

A thorough believer of kindness and respect for all and a strict follower of the personal motto;

"Be yourself, because everyone else is taken."

His book aims to spread the love and awareness to the animals. He grew up surrounded by multiple working dogs what contributed to shaping his personality. This book speaks volumes about his bond with dogs.

The harsh cold winds of winter were unbearable. The little stream running down the mountain slope looked magical as the full moon shone its light down on it, it was as if inside a fairy-tale. The banks of the stream were frozen, and pebbles below could be seen through the hazy mirror of stream water. Some as sharp as needles, but almost all as smooth as silk. An Eagle Owl rustled in the pine leaves, letting out an alarming 'hoot-hoot' at the sound of a distant pack of wolves howling into the night. Their tracks were now probably being covered up by the rapidly falling snow. The susurration of stream was hummed down as the snow glaciated the stream halfway.

The cave was murky and felt very cold, while its floor shimmered thanks to the puddles. I stood at the entrance, the wind howling in my ears. A blanket of snow covered the ground and the many pine trees that grew tall and strong behind me. I was here looking for a sheep, which had jumped its paddock fence. I was out patrolling the area when I saw it in the distance, running off far to the mountains.

A lump of brown hair was closing in around the horrified sheep. Oh, my God! I thought, am I too late!? Trembling with fear and hyperventilating in fear, I had no idea what to do. I knew that a brown bear was roaming around the Tatra Mountains during this time of the year. I wandered about the cave, looking for a clue that would lead me to the dumb woolly animal. Just moments later, I heard a noise. It was a distressed 'baa'... and clip-clopping of hooves moving back and forth time and time again.

Will I be able to save this sheep? Can we even make it out of here alive? Oh, my God! I rushed forwards eagerly until I reached a cave junction. *Which way do I go?* I hesitated. In the distance, I heard the commotion continue. *Am I too late? Has the beast feasted?* I knew I had to act fast, but I was unable to find a smell due to the half-eaten deer that lay on the floor. Its scent was potent and covered up the one I was looking for so desperately.

Pricking my ears, I tried my best to get some sense of where the sheep were presently based. From the tunnel up ahead, the racket went on. I proceeded with my small mission. After ten minutes of walking about, I had finally arrived at the scene, and just in time too. A lump of brown hair was closing in around the horrified sheep. I had to act fast.

The bear was just about the attack. I barked with all my might. It came thundering from my slobbery mouth ferociously and passed throughout the cave.

The bear turned around, rose upon me, and growled. "Looks like I'll be having a burger for dinner!" Instantly, he swiped his massive paw at me.

Jumping off the cave wall, I dodged the attack, landed behind him, and finished with a harsh growl back. The bear turned around. *Okay, now he is going to have me as a feast. Think, think of something!* All that harsh training and significant genes seem to be of no use. I started questioning everything and my very existence and purpose of being the guard of the herd. He was closing around us again. I leaped forward and scratched his muzzle with my claws, which, luckily, haven't been trimmed yet. The front part of his body fell to the ground as he covered the lesion. I snapped at the sheep's hooves and herded it out of the cave and back to its home. I was tired afterward. So tired that I could barely walk back home. The stress and tension of the rescue must have been the cause of this feeling. *Nothing a little rest can't cure*, I thought to myself as I staggered up the steep mountain. When I arrived at my house's wooden door, I sat down, then lifted my paw to it, leaving a tiny scratch. The scratch looked deeper next to the old ones.

Scratching the door was something that I always had done to warn my owner, Klimek, I was back from my 'side jobs' now and then. Klimek is a thirty-year-old, good-heightened guy with outstanding brown eyes and a curved nose right above the goodness-filled smile that lingers on his lips almost all the time. He was my best friend and work-partner! Of course, he and I would go along with five other people for my big rescues. We work as volunteers. Our Mountain Rescue is a volunteer-run. We all do this from the goodness of our hearts. We are relying only on donations of people who only wish for good. Putting our lives at risk all the time, but we ask for no recognition. The feeling you have, knowing that you saved someone's life, is unbelievable. Well, you could also say that we were adrenaline seekers to be fair.

A few days after my little escapade, we got a call. A call for help. A need for rescue. A rescue of a lost snowboarder who had been vanished... Parted from the rest of his club. They'd been boarding down near the Sleeping Knight Mountain. This place is exceedingly high, so we all had to go on a helicopter to get there. I have rehearsed for extreme situations. Long hours of hard drills to get used to being lowered on the line down the helicopter.

Scent work was my favourite, though. The rescue missions do sound exciting and thrilling, but it is only exciting if you know how to make it out alive with the person stuck in hazard. It's a training scenario, but the challenges are very real.

The sleet is typical of the weather Mountain Rescue teams get called out in, and we're moving up a slope through rough vegetation surrounded by loose stone boulders. It's exactly where missing persons tend to be. Either they've fallen, tucked away trying to shelter from the prevailing weather, got lost and wandered away from known paths, or they're vulnerable. Sometimes people who might be trying to conceal themselves intentionally. The route of the search and rescue team is not easy – rugged terrain, in the worst of weather.

I started my training as a very young dog I have spent days of training hunt for a missing person. We are trained to detect scent in the air, rather than follow a scent trail on the ground. Every minute humans shed some 40,000 particles of skin, sweat, bacteria and other body products. These are carried on the wind, floating away from their bodies, diffusing a signature into the air. Once a person is stationary, the scent will spread downwind in a cone shape.

With a sense of smell 100 times more sensitive than a human's, our nose-my nose is a life-saving tool. The dog handler's job is to take into account topography and wind direction, and send the dog across the search area in such a way that they have the best chance of coming across the "scent cone".

The handler's job is also to ensure every successful search is rewarded. Therefore the end of the search is what we are looking forward to the most. It is obvious, life-saving is very rewarding but a squeaky toy in the shape of a burger is what we love.

Human's life depends on me and my handler, Klimek, and for this rescue, I had to put that special training into use. Once we arrived at the place where the snowboarding group had last seen their lost member, my team lowered me down, and Klimek unclipped us both. Almost instantly after that, I began my search. I sniffed the ground, trying to pick up the scent of the man. Within minutes, I found it. It was a smell of boots, gloves, sweat, and cologne! Leading up ahead was a trail of footprints. A man's prints which meant he lost his snowboard and tried to walk.

The snowboarder! I thought to myself excitedly. *It had to be!* I ran along. My heart was thudding in my chest rapidly at the suspense of the mission. The fragrance was getting stronger. *I am getting there*! A blue dot in the distance was visible now. It had to be the top of his boot sticking out from underneath the snow. The man, indeed, at this point, could not move a muscle. I ran over to where he lay. We dug him out as fast as we could. Once he was out, Klimek examined him. The snowboarder was cold and barely able to move or speak. He had a broken leg and was losing consciousness. Klimek opened the small barrel that hung just under my collar and poured whisky into the man's mouth to save him from the danger of awaiting death. Alcohol warms up the body from the inside out, creating a warmer body temperature. If we had started from the outside, raising his body temperature too rapidly, he could have lost his limbs. After Klimek had made a splint out of the sticks he found lying on the ground, he called for the helicopter using his walkie-talkie to pick us up. This time with 'cargo.'

While we were waiting for the helicopter to arrive, I saw something in the distance. It seemed to be heading in our direction. Something huge. Brown. It was standing on four legs. I realised that it was the same bear from before. I guess he still didn't learn the lesson.

When he had come close enough and stood on his two hind legs, he growled at me, "You!" baring his teeth.

"We have some unfinished business to attend to!" I barked back at him in an attempt to scare him off.

I have a long line of ancestors who were able to do so! He replied to me with another harsh roar. Harsher than before. I heard Klimek and the snowboarder behind me shuffling backwards in fright.

I could sense, I could smell their fear; knowing how scared they were, I lunged towards the bear and attacked it with all I had. My jaws opened up, and I clenched them around the bear's neck. I shook my head relentlessly, trying to injure him enough to leave. He threw himself onto his back, forcing me to let go for a moment, before immediately jumping to his feet! He towered over me. And after a while, landed on all four paws. He raised his right paw sideways above the ground and brutally swiped it across my abdomen. The snow stained red underneath me.

The scratches caused severe pain. I felt fear myself now. Fear that I would die. Fear that Klimek would no longer have someone to take care of him any more…I love this man so dearly. I tried to ignore my pain and forced myself to stand up once more. Before the bear could react, I reached out and scratched him as hard as I could, across the left eye. He yelled out in shock and pain as he turned his head away, thus giving me a clear place to bite him. The bear ran off, leaving a trail of blood behind him. Just before he disappeared, he looked back at me. I thought I could see respect in his eyes. Had we fought our last fight?

Huffing and puffing with all my might as every breath I took weighed on me. My legs trembled, and my heartbeat echoed in my ears. It was anger coupled with fear and ignited by the thrill of standing tall in a fight against a bear. I turned my attention towards Klimek, and the rescued human and both of them had expressions brimming with gratitude and shock. I could almost read what they both were saying in their heads.

After a while the snowboarder murmured breathlessly, "This dog has guts! Wait till I tell the others, but I certainly must say; never in my life, saw a human become as pale as you."

Klimek looked towards him, and both laughed nervously, still unable to comprehend what exactly has just happened. Klimek heart almost burst from the amount of love he felt for me. Soon after that, the helicopter arrived. Paramedics took the man on the stretcher, then Klimek and I went back with the team via our helicopter.

This mission was so frightening; it left a mark in our memories for life. Yet, it has never stopped us from working. I healed, and we continued our knee-jerking rescues. These are the real deal rescue missions, so full of danger and excitement. I loved it and wouldn't want it any other way. I felt so accomplished after every each of them. I went home knowing that I saved someone's life, rescued them from the fear of the depths of an avalanche. I did something useful and meaningful.

Living where Klimek and I did, we barely ever saw anyone besides the deer and other wildlife critters. The only people we ever saw were the people who lived in town when we would go to get the groceries from the store or collect the mail. Life was plentiful there; I was well fed, Klimek always showed love and affection, and I had a nice soft bed to sleep next to the fireplace.

As the saying goes "nothing lasts forever," I never knew I would have to experience the truth it holds. One day, all that faded away…I've been sent to the animal rescue down in Krakow. Klimek got into an accident. It happened on his way back from his girlfriend's house. He had just proposed to her during a romantic dinner. He must have been so happy and full of hope. I had listened to him to prepare a speech for this special moment. He worked on it all the night before to make sure he didn't mess up the words. All the time he was preparing for it, I laid on the living room rug bored out of my mind.

I never liked his girlfriend. I only met her once, but my dog's intuition never had anything good to say about her. Every time I heard her name, I wanted to bark as much as I could, trying to tell him not to do it. She is not right for you. The next thing I've heard, he was on his motorbike, tearing down the narrow mountain road. After taking a sharp turn, the last thing he expected was a grey wolf to be crossing the road. He revved his engine in an attempt to scare it off but was unable to do so. Not to hurt the undomesticated canine, he swerved out of the way, almost instantly tumbling down the hill, tearing a hole on his left trouser leg and in the elbows of his leather jacket. Scrapes all over his body. He made it out alive.

However, I can't say the same for his bike. It had banged against multiple trees, splitting it into plenty of sharp pieces that managed to fling into Klimek's chest and hip, creating a world of pain for him. The ambulance took him to the hospital, unconscious. Doctors kept him there for months while I was under the care of his brother, Derek. Soon, I overheard the chat that Derek and his wife were having, learning that Klimek could not do many of the things he usually could. The doctors told him that his injuries were more severe than they had previously thought, and they have to keep him longer. There was also no guarantee that he would fully recover physically.

Knowing this, his newly become fiancé left him all alone to deal with the pain. She said, or mostly yelled – "I will not start married life with a cripple!"

What a horrible thing to say and do. But there was no surprise to me. I could sense her rotten soul for a long time. Way before anyone could spot it! After that, Klimek was lonely and depressed. He didn't eat the food that nurses provided, no matter how much they pleaded.

Staying longer meant that I would not see him any time soon. And I needed someone to look after me. Klimek didn't have many friends, and the ones he did have, lived in other countries or were too busy with their jobs or families. My work team was not keen on working with me in Klimek's absence, and Derek and his wife were too busy to deal with three young children to take on such a big dog. Derek didn't have any other choice than to take me to the shelter hoping that I will have a second chance in life. With another family. I did not hold it against him. I knew it breaks his heart to see me go.

I hopped into the trunk of the car. Derek started to drive. And as he did, I thought about Klimek and how I would probably never see him again. I blamed it all on that stupid grey wolf. Why did it have to be crossing the road at the same time as Klimek? It's all his fault!

But I regretted later on all that I had thought. I knew that I was mad and had no one else to take it out on, other than that wolf. I laid down and closed my eyes, trying to comfort myself with happy thoughts. I soon fell asleep, waking up only to find the car at a full stop. I rose up from my belly and looked out through the large back window of the 2007 Honda CR-V.

After we arrived at Krakow Animal Rescue Centre, Derek asked one of the animal shelter workers to help him get me out of the car. He was in tears; I knew what he meant by asking for help.
The man, who came helping, was dressed in dark green cargo clothing and had a lead attached to the uniform's belt. He clipped the lead onto my brown, leather collar with a small, barrel-shaped name tag. Then, he led me to my enclosure. It was a large cage with a wooden house at the back that I could go into any time of the day. On the right side of the

door, two tin bowls hung low to the ground. The bowl closest to the door was half-filled with water. My mouth felt dry; it had been a long journey. I turned and lowered my head down to the bowl. Water sloshed everywhere as my tongue curled up around it and transported the liquid into my mouth.

Derek knelt in front of me; the bars separated us. He reached his arm in through one of the gaps and scratched my neck tenderly. "Bye bud," he said and went back to his car.

Every step he took away from those bars confirmed me that this shelter home would be my place of dwelling now. That was the last I ever saw of him. My life and everything I knew, everything I learned and everything I was habituated with got torn away from me.

***

I was placed at the end of the enclosures, next to an old German shepherd who never seemed to interact with the humans much.

"My name's Shepherd," he told me in his low, croaky voice, "What's yours?"

"My name's Buck... How long have you been here?" I responded. Shepherd chuckled lightly. I hadn't had the slightest idea what amused him so much.

He replied, "I've been staying in this kennel for over six years! They say that we don't know the concept of time." He murmured and turned his head away.

"What do these humans know!?" I asked.

"Huh, that's a pretty long time." Shepherd murmured. There was a pause after that.

"So, how do you get picked?" I questioned.

"What?" A perplexed exclamation was all he had in response.

"You know, like, do you act all cute and cuddly, or do you act all tough and scary? I mean, for someone to take you home." I tried elaborating my question.

"Boy, haven't you ever been chosen by a human before?" murmured Shepherd.

"Well, yeah, but the last time I have been, I was like, nine weeks old! I know only one place where I belonged." The heaviness of not belonging to this started to settle in me. At this point, I felt like my throat is getting squeezed by the upcoming waterfall of tears. I swallowed it down and stood with my head up.
"O'kay, well, I can't tell you, and I haven't ever been chosen. I was born on the streets!" He rumbled and turned around to go back to his hut but stopped just before entering. "Try acting like yourself; see if that works!" he called back, "Night Buck!"

"Night," I replied.

Before going to bed, I realised that this was the first time I've been away from Klimek for this long since he got me. As the stars twinkled up in the night sky, I sat wondering what Klimek would be doing at this moment and whether he was thinking of me, the way I was thinking of him. I sniffled my hushed cries and tried to catch forty winks to look good and healthy enough for people coming to the shelter house for pets.

Monday morning rose, and with it came people looking for the perfect dog to take home. Plenty of people came walking past my enclosure. An old, rich looking lady strode up to my kennel and looked down at me interestedly; she stood there longer than anyone else did. The lady wore a pink dress and a white pearl necklace and carried a small handbag that hung from her shoulder. Inside it sat a little golden furred Chihuahua. The woman and her dog soon went walking away. *Spoilt looking dog* I thought. *I'm glad they're both gone!* But I was wrong. SOOO wrong. According to the little Chihuahua, the old lady, who was named Kate, came up to one of the workers beside the Manager's office door. This was the worker who usually fed and walked me.

"I think I found a dog I would like!" Kate said, gesturing her hand to me in a posh way.

"You did? Great, so, would you like to come inside? The Manager will help with the paperwork," the worker helped her with the rest of the procedures.

About an hour later, Kate and the Manager, who I had seen for the first time, exited the room laughing. They must have been joking about something because adopting a dog isn't usually something you laugh about. Feeling joy-yes, but laughing- not really. Both of them shook hands and thanked each other kindly.

"Would you like help to take the dog to your ca… I mean limo," he said in amazement, staring at the long, recently washed vehicle.

"No, thank you!" she replied, "I'll have one of my servants do that!" Servants! It doesn't even sound right!

Where my previous owner was a self-employed carpenter and passionate volunteer, my next owner was going to be the elite with servants to carry their stuff around. From a humble and down-to-earth handler like Klimek to the woman of extravagance, I was about to experience the most drastic change in my life.

***

Arriving at Kate's home, the butler opened the door for me. I hopped out and came to see the largest house I had ever seen. Inside, all the floors were tiled in black and white, and the ceiling was built high above everyone's heads with a large golden chandelier hanging off it. Old paintings filled all the house walls. Kate's ancestors and the little Chihuahua called Rickey were framed in them. In the kitchen, at least five chefs cooked dinner and dessert; the smell made me feel as if I was in heaven. As I ventured throughout the house, the more I looked around, the greater my bewilderment became. The living room was brilliant, the bathrooms were beautiful, and the beds were the best ones I have seen. While mooning about in the house I realised something. There were six rooms, one as a dressing room, one as a dog playroom, one as a gym (which I was about to discover no one ever use), one as an indoor garden for when it's raining outside, and only two bedrooms.

"Where the hell am I supposed to sleep?" I questioned this aloud, hoping that someone would answer me. Rickey came scurrying along, like the most pampered squirrel ever.

"Who? You?! Ha, you get to sleep on the floor downstairs, you don't need a bed, and you don't deserve one. Besides, you'd make a hole in it anyway. You'd wreck the whole room too!" He turned back the way he came from. "Do us all a favour and go back to the streets where you belong. Kate only needs one dog. And that dog is me!" The condescending sneer was the last thing I heard as he headed back to where he came from.

Evening came. Kate got us ready for bed while one of the servants laid a blue plush bed for me in the living room, washed me, prepared a water bowl by my side and left. On his way out, switched the light off; leaving me alone in the dark. Only the mysterious moon to accompany me. The silence deepened as the moon reached its high point in the sky. The morning must be around the corner; there was certain consolation in seeing the moon resting at its crowning point.

The morning light shone through the window, waking me up from my dreams—the thing I always hated unless there was a long day of playing ahead of me. I rose from my bed, and in my imagination, I was expecting him to be in the kitchen making breakfast. I went to the kitchen, but only to see the chefs milling around, obviously. Klimek was nowhere to be seen. And then it struck me, I remembered what had happened. I remembered about his crash…yeah…I remembered it all. I got out of this depressed state and made way to the living room. A while later, Kate entered the room, wearing a black silk night mask raised up on her head and holding Rickey in her short arms before placing him down on the floor. "Morning, err …" Ricky stammered.

"Buck, my name's Buck!" I got angry.

"Whatever. What do you want for breakfast?" he continued with his questions without paying any heed to my frustration.

"Gee, I don't know. What's to offer?" I answered, completely clueless.

"Nothing, you don't get to choose. Only Kate chooses! And it's always the same thing. Kibble!" he told me, in a disliked tone. I ignored this.

Five minutes later, the breakfast was served. The servant shovelled it from the food bucket and into our bowls. When he had finished, I dug in.

"Eh-hmm!" Ricky coughed forcefully.

I looked up. "Can I help you?" I asked.

"You're eating from my bowl!" he snapped back.

I scoffed, "What's the difference?"

"The difference is that one is shiny and new looking, and the other one- isn't!"

"And?" His reply had me flabbergasted.

"AND-" he mimicked and continued, "I deserve the shiny one. You don't."

This little guy was so conceited he'd never believe that anyone should get a better bowl of food than the one he's had. These nasty remarks against me one by one filled me up with rage. But I tried to withhold my anger. So, I moved over to the other bowl. From boastful and egoistic comments to his annoying strutting, everything about Ricky made me enraged at his every existence.

"Happy now?" I remarked and followed what he said.

"Yes, thank you 'Shmuck'!" the haughtiness was this guy was unbelievable.

"It's Buck!" I corrected him with suppressed anguish.

"Don't care!" Snarled Ricky.

It wasn't the first or last time that Rickey tried to get on my nerves. And I wondered *why he is like this? Is he jealous of me, or is it simply his rude character?* Never found out.

Days passed by. All the same routine. Boredom, mixed with the unpleasantness of Ricky. I became used to of his rudeness and tried to habituate myself with this new house and my so-called new masters. The shiny bowl was still Ricky's possession, and his strut and arrogant gait became an everyday thing for me. Almost two months after I arrived, I was still tortured by the tiny dog.

One evening; Kate obviously with the pearls on, Rickey, and I were watching the news on TV. I savoured this time, as only then the Chihuahua, who was undoubtedly cursed by Satan, did not bully me. Yet, I was going to be in for a real surprise. Ricky had his plan in mind. Once Kate left the salon for the loo, Ricky hopped up on the orange seat which Kate had been sitting on. Seconds later, a strange smell drifted across the room. The malodour was almost intolerable. I moved over to where Rickey sat.

"Hey Rickey, do you smell that?" I hated to ask him this. Well, I hated to ask him anything.

"No!" he responded to my question, then he bounced off and ran away towards the kitchen.

Strange! I thought. I could swear this is the smell of something we should only do outdoors! The smell still wandered around my head and made the entire room stink. It became impossible to concentrate on the TV.

I jumped up onto the arm of the chair, my back paws glued to the floor, keeping me balanced. Something dark coloured laid curled up there--what was making that appalling smell disgusted me. *Rickey pooped on Kate's chair! I knew something was up. I knew it!* That was the moment when Kate entered back into the room. She gave me a gentle pat on my head before sitting back down.

"NO!" I barked, trying to stop her.

"Oh, stop it!" She shushed away my yelps and woofs.

My attempts to stop her were useless, for she would never understand. She didn't have that connection that Klimek and I had. He always knew what I meant to tell him. It was almost as if he could speak dog language. The woman proceeded to sit, and as she sat down completely, an unpleasant squish filled the air in the room. She stood up again.

"UGH!" she exclaimed. "Did you do this?!"

"No!" I barked again, but my protests were to no avail.

Kate took me by my new collar, which she had ordered from a German designer, and dragged me outside to the garden.

"Now you stay here and think about what you've done!" This was the last straw.

I don't belong here. I do not want to spend the rest of my life feeling unsafe in my own home! As I spent my time outside, I planned an escape. An escape that I would succeed in doing at night, while Kate and Rickey would be asleep.

Night came, and it was time to put my plan into action. I got up from my blue bed and tried to silently make my way to the hall, without making noise with my nails. The right time to utilize stealth mode training. Two male servants were talking near the entrance to the back yard. I was going to have to sneak past them to get there. Looking around, I found a squeaky tennis ball, or in other words, the perfect diversion! I picked it up in my mouth and carried it briskly to the other side of the corridor. I was lucky that no one saw me. I compressed the ball in my mouth, making it squeak. I made a dash to hide behind one of the cupboards. The men came to the area where I had squeaked the ball and looked around. One of them looked down and picked up the light green sphere. They stayed there, discussing how strange it was, and they swore that they heard something, but no one was there. I sneaked past them and went outside through the large doggy doors that Kate had ordered from some posh place to fit my size.

Outside, I scanned the area and found the perfect spot to dig under the fence. After working out and securing my escape route, I paused and decided to one last thing before I leave this torture house forever. I went over to Ricky's outdoor water bowl and stuck my right paw in it, making it dirty and filled with lumpy black soil. This was a way of saying, *Drink dirt, Rickey!* I never liked that dog, from the moment I met him, I knew he was going to be an annoying little brat. So, that night, I walked back to the animal shelter, asking directions from the stray dogs of Krakow; they knew their way through the city way better than anyone else did. I had to admit the way back to the shelter house was not an easy one, from wrong directions to encountering troublesome street dogs. Around an hour later, I arrived at the shelter house. They were just about to close up for the night. When the keeper saw me, his face lit up, followed by a change of expression to sheer disbelief. He liked me, and I liked him too.

"I thought you got a new home", he said to me. *Yeah well, things change*! I thought, and he walked me to the kennel where I had stayed before. In the morning, Shepherd came out of his doghouse, realising I was there. He stared at me in shock.

"You are back!" he said, confused. "I thought you left with that lady and her Chihuahua!" he added.

"Well, I did, and now I'm back!" I replied with a bit more sadness laden with anger.

"Really?" He chuckled lightly before continuing his sentence, "How did you pull that one off?"

"You don't want to know." He chuckled again; the conversation ended there.

He greedily ate his food placed by one of the workers. He licked his bowl empty quickly; it was as if they didn't feed him for days. The shelter house became a safe haven and Shepherd the companion of good and bad days.

***

Even though that house offered nothing more than feeling of strangeness, the prospect of being 'home' would often cloud my thoughts. The days after that were long and boring. And the nights, even more so. It had been a week since I had escaped from Kate and Ricky's house. It was the worst week I've ever had, and I began to doubt that I'm ever going to have a family again. I missed Klimek so much. It was not just the feeling of fondness that he had for me; it was the knowledge of having someone to take care of me that made me devoted to him.

Two days later, the animal shelter had another open day, where families came from all over the place to see the dogs, who, if they're lucky, could be taken home. I couldn't say I was excited since the last time someone chose me as their pet; it didn't end well. The excitement of getting adopted and having a family were overpowered by the fear of being mistreated once again. Once again, someone came up to my kennel door and stared at me. I avoided to stare back, but it was too irresistible. I just had to see how these people looked. It was a little girl this time. She reached in and stroked my fur; I didn't refuse to let her do it; I loved the way she petted me. She giggled and called her parents.

"Mum, dad! Come look at this dog, he's adorable!" The girl clamoured.

She couldn't have been any older than six. She was too small to be, and her voice was too squeaky. The two adults came towards their child and stood next to her. After a few minutes of hard thinking, they finally decided. They filled out the same paperwork Kate had to and were conclusively ready to take me home. Another quest to find a family, to call someone's place my home, to experience the fondness of an affectionate master…one more pursuit, one more adventure of life.

To be completely honest, I was a little nervous about going home with these people for two reasons. One, the first time someone took me home from the animal shelter, it was a horrible experience. Remember Ricky? And two, this is the first time that I'm going to live in the same household as a little child, I was scared that I would accidentally hurt her. After all, I am a giant breed and let's face it, a little clumsy.

The family took me home. I expected to see a gigantic mansion just like the old lady Kate but much to my surprise, their house was not much bigger than Klimek's log cabin up in the Tatra Mountains. Inside, it was spotless. Cleaner than Klimek's hut ever was. It had stairs which led to the second floor, where there were a bathroom and two bedrooms—one for Eva, and the other for her parents. As I found out later that day, I was going to be sleeping in Eva's room, and this was much better than sleeping alone in the living room.

The morning sun rose like it always did, and everyone woke up for breakfast. Eva (the little girl) and her parents bought dog food on the way back from the rescue. They also bought me a unique looking food bowl and a collar both had my name on it. The food wasn't as good as the one Kate had to offer, but one thing's for sure, they had shown me more affection than she ever did. I embraced my new place in life. Eva's unceasing kindness and her parents' thorough care assured me that I would be taken care of.

Eva's dad, Ian, was the one who usually took me for walks, and sometimes Eva tagged along too. It is a lot better to have someone to take you for walks, instead of some strange dog walker that you don't know. The feeling of affinity can make all the difference when it comes to walking your dog.

Another reason to dislike rich people, the thought got registered in my mind. After spending lots of time with Eva, I soon learned everything about her. She was the only child, she was allergic to peanuts, her favourite animals were dogs, and she loved to draw. There was more, but this is what is most important about her. I realised that there was no need to be afraid of this family. The place felt safe, and I was appreciated there.

One day, I was out on a walk with Eva's dad. Walking down the neighbourhood road, I looked across the street. A striped, ginger cat sat on one of the house windowsills. It was one that always made fun of me, kind of like how Rickey did, but less offensively, I guess. Whenever this cat saw me, he'd laugh and call me a 'Freak!'--the worst cat ever. Not that any cats are precisely the best pet to keep...If you know what I mean. I learnt to ignore "Smelly cat" as much as possible, but this time, he also said terrible things about my new family. Hearing his sneering remarks made me agitated. Tugging at my lead with all my strength, I pulled it out of the man's hand, and ran straight across the street, eager to get the evil feline. He leapt off of the windowsill in fright.

Before I was able to make it across to the other side, a car came speeding over the hill. The next thing I knew, I was on the road, unable to move. Ian came running into the middle of the road and knelt to examine me. The man who drove the vehicle got out of the car.

"Oh God!" he said, almost apologetically. "I'm so sorry, I…Is there anything I can do?" For a little while, there was no answer.

"Yes, can you please drive us to the vet?!" Eva's dad replied in utter shock.

"Sure, I will help you load the dog in!" The guilty man then drove us to the closest vet.

All I can remember is Eva's dad asking the vet how bad I was and how much will it cost to fix me up. "Surgery will need to be involved!" the vet explained. Ian asked how expensive the surgery was going to be.

I must have passed out again as the next thing I witnessed was resting in my kennel at the animal rescue. In front of me, Eva was crying as she knelt and stuck her arm through the bars again. To say goodbye, like Derek did once. I didn't understand what was going on. I tried to get up. But soon fell back down; the car hurt my back-left paw.

Now as I started to put the puzzles together, it all made sense. *Money! The good and the evil of the human race. People have this saying "Money doesn't give happiness." Yet here I am, just because of ...money.* Ian could not afford my treatment, so he did the next best thing, he could think of. Eva and her parents walked away, I could tell, they didn't want to, and honestly, I did not want to lose them either. The feeling of being torn away from my family grew more intense as I knew the injury might have lasting impacts.

Later that day, the shelter set up a 'Go Fund Me Page' for people to send donations that would pay for my leg surgery. I was sad and in pain asking myself one question over and over; "Why does money mean so much to people? Why their entire existence relies on money." Such questions kept me worried and sleepless at nights. The thought of being without family for the rest of life would haunt me, worsening my mental state.

Christmas was clearly approaching. I could smell it in the air. Christmas lights were put up all over the place. Usually, I would love this time of the year. Klimek and I would work a lot and then I would rest my head on his lap in front of the fireplace, while he sang me traditional Christmas carols. He wasn't the best singer, but to hear his voice and see how happy he was, would always be an honour. Yet now, I was sad and lonely, almost sure nothing good awaits for me anymore. The month of joys and unending celebration turned into the worst time of life—a period of perpetual sorrow and loneliness. Left alone in my kennel at animal rescue, this Christmas was nothing about presents, celebrations, carols but needles, medicines and pain, lots and lots of pain.

One evening they took us for a walk, the weather has turned slightly chilly, but the cold was bearable. I looked into the sky, observed the very first snowflakes fall onto the ground. Cold and refreshing. Back at my kennel, I sat outside and watched them fall more and more as the snow layer on ground thickened with every blow of snow-filled air. After looking for a while, I soon found a snowflake that looked almost perfectly-- symmetrical from all sides and proportional from all angles. It was as if it didn't want to fall on the ground, as it stayed levitating near my muzzle. I watched it and wished; *I wished to be happy again. To find a home where I would matter and belong.* If only my wish could be granted this way. A single tear dropped out of my eye. I was not in the right place mentally. My mind was sorrowful. We all were losing hope, and my leg was still in pain. A couple more days passed before something happened.

A kind family, who wasn't rich nor poor, but had just enough money and heart to make a donation that would pay of the vet bill entirely. I remember how happy everyone was. That day I went back to the vet, where they gave me an anaesthetic to make me sleep through the surgery.

Just a short while later, I was back at the shelter. Well, in my timekeeping someone wrapped up my hurt paw in a dark blue bandage. I tried standing up, and much to my surprise, I was almost capable. It still hurt and I was shaky but much less than earlier. Turning my glance away from the leg, I fixed it on the kennel next to me. Shepherd laid there close to the wired fence splitting us up. He didn't move a muscle. Away from him, his food bowl was full. Unusual of him.

"Shepherd?" I spoke. There was no answer.

"Shepherd, are you okay?" There wasn't a sound from any direction. I investigated.

The moon produced just enough light for me to see the other canines. They too laid in their kennel, food bowls full, even Noodles, a tiny Corgi. All as still as a rock. A panic arose in my heart. Behind me, I felt a presence. I turned around. It was Klimek. Joy and relief captured my panic for the moment. I barked and sprinted towards the man. But before leaping on him. Something happened.

He fell to his knees. It was as if he was an elderly man. When he stood up, I could see that he had morphed into a different figure. Evilly cackling, he appeared much more massive than he ever was. It wasn't Klimek anymore, but a dark shadow. The shadow bent over me and let out another cackle. I tucked my fluffy tail between my legs and crouched lower as I moved back in fear, letting out a whimper as my hind hit the coop gate. I had nowhere to go. And nowhere to hide. The shadow closed in around me. It was creating darkness around me. One more step closer, and he swallowed me in his largemouth.

I opened my eyes, panting like crazily. I calmed myself down as I understood that everything that had just happened was a dream. Just a terrible nightmare. Probably the side effects of anaesthetic given to me for the surgery. Gradually, I realized that I was in a house. Not Klimek's house. Not Kate's or Eva's. I was in a place that I was not familiar with.

In front of me, a strange little girl was staring at me, curiously.

Her little brown eyes were so full of wonder and life.

"Mum, Dad, Al! Come! The dog's up," she yelled.

They all came rushing into the room and knelt around me, stretching their arms one at a time for me to smell them—all except one. It was a boy, a ten-year-old boy as I found out. He stood there, arms crossed, as he gave me a menacing look and quickly turned his eyes to look outside through the window.

I tried standing up, and much to my surprise, I was able to. I looked back at my hurt paw, and it was bandaged, but not with a blue bandage, like in the dream, but with a red one. I began walking toward the boy. The rest of the family moved away, leaving me a free path. I started sniffing him and nuzzled his hand affectionately. But he completely brushed me off. The boy, Al or Alex for long, left the room instantly. The two parents followed to see what was troubling the boy. As it turned out, Alex had always wanted a German Shepherd, like Shepherd, my friend from the animal shelter. But, this was different from what his little sister, Mia, wanted. She never cared what breed she would have; all she ever wanted was a dog that she could hug and play with. A couple of months passed by, and I learned more about the family and connected with them on a new level. Besides Alex... I could not go through to him; I could not reach out to him in whatever was troubling him. The only thing I got to know about him is that he's into karate.

There was a tournament being held in that coming week that

excited him greatly. He had trained all year for that competition and was sure he could win this time. He learned every move and trick in the book and was all set and prepared to lift the shining trophy.

It was the day—the day of the tournament. I had to stay home because apparently, dogs aren't allowed in the building. It didn't matter. Soon I knew, he did not win seeing his reaction back at home. He entered the house, quickly placed his trophy on the table and ran upstairs to his room, slamming it harshly behind him. I went to the table and read the engraved writing, *'Under 18's championship; Third place.'* The rest of the family left him alone for a while so that he can express and let out his frustration and emotion in privacy. I couldn't see him like this, even though he didn't like me; I made my way up the stairs. Somehow, I managed to open the door, by standing on my back paws and using my front ones to push down the handle. I entered,

"Go away!" he said angrily, raising his head. "Oh, it's you!"

I came closer to the bed and looked him in the eyes. He turned his head to the other side. I sat there, and I wouldn't leave; not until he felt better. After a while, he turned his head back to face me. I lowered my head and rested it on the bed, letting out a small whimper. He stretched out his arm and gently patted me. The next day, Alex was in the back yard, practising his kata, the base of karate. I joined him outside.

"Go, I need to train; there's another tournament in a couple of days. It's even more important," he continued with his insistence. But once again, I didn't leave.

After a while, I decided to join him. I was trying to stand on my hind legs and practice the kata with him. I almost instantly failed. Alex chuckled.

"What?" he questioned, "You like karate too?" I barked as a reply. He took this as a yes, and quickly ran inside. It took a while, but when he came back out, he was holding a black headband in his hand.

"Come here, boy" I came closer, and he tied the band around my head and said, "There, now you're a karate dog!" and that moment changed everything.

The next karate tournament came quicker than we thought. The entire family prepared to attend the event, and once again, the dogs weren't allowed. I could not go, but I was promised by both children to get a full report of events. So it happened.

The first match was easy for Alex. But as he kept on fighting and progressing the tournament, it got harder and harder, especially during the finals. But it was all worth it in the end because when he came home, he held in his hand the trophy for the winner of first position. He was throwing jab punches, blocking the opponent's attacks and much more while celebrating his victory. Both the parents loved Al's 'thank you speech' in which he mentioned me. He thanked me, his best friend! That was what I had been waiting for. This was one of the happiest days of my life.

Finally! A true family. True friends and a sense of purpose in my life once again. The sense of belongingness, which had been a major missing in the past few years, was regained A few months passed after the tournament, and we were all sitting in front of the TV watching 'Bugs Bunny, Mia's favourite show. That was when we heard a knock on the door. Mia and Alex went to answer the door. What they saw was a tall gentleman with a wooden cane, who asked if a big, white-haired dog lived here. The questions from a strange man made both siblings a little confused and uneasy. Hearing the man's voice, and snuffling a little of this unique scent, I rushed towards the door as fast as I could. The good part was that by then I could run the same speed as before because a few days ago, I had my leg cast removed. I jumped up onto the man and started licking his face.

It was Klimek! Yes, yes! Now he was using a walking stick, but other than that, he was the same person. He was my Klimek! Mia and Al's parents came running to the door after hearing the commotion. Seeing me lick Klimek, they decided to invite him inside. The couple recognised that there is a story between us and trusted their dog's sense. Klimek explained to them quickly how he was my former owner, and how I used to be a search and rescue dog up in the Tatra Mountains. The meeting put my certain behavioural traits and characteristics in a new light to my family. Digging was not much appreciated by Mia, and so far she could not understand why.

After two long hours of talking, many cups of coffee and a traditional apple cake, Klimek and my new family made a plan. They decided that it would be good for Klimek to come over every other weekend just so, he and I spend some time together like how we used to do. It was a dream come true. After all the sadness and lonely days, we could be together once more. Somewhat different than before, but we both grew older and got richer in one or two experiences more;

therefore, we were keen to accept the new reality. The reality that was the best of both worlds. I had more love one could ever ask for-- both from Klimek and my new and forever family.

Sometimes, we all go up to the Tatra Mountains and rent a little cabin from this very nice lady, who also owns a Polish Tatra Sheepdog, just like me. Only it's a female, and her name's Jessica. She has lived with the lady, also known as Hanka, for as long as I can remember. Jessika has the same bond with Hanka as I had with Klimek.

It's very joyful to be back in the mountains. It brings me back to the times of my rescuing career. I love this feeling of sweet memories.

Two years on, from our first family visit to the mountains to meet Klimek, I have found out that Jessica just had given birth to my four daughters and four sons. I knew that soon they would have to go on their own little life journey, but only the fact that I was a father, made me very proud and fulfilled. My daughter, Arabella, out of all the pups, reminded me of myself the most. I have the feeling that she still may encounter the same journey as I did-- becoming a Mountain Rescue dog.

And that's it. That's the story of how I got a fantastic life. Every fortnight is now a huge celebration for me-- a celebration of love and friendship that beats all the odds. I could tell you much more about my experiences, but I will keep it to myself. Until the next time we meet. For now, I tell you this before we part. Every Christmas, I look up into the sky and howl a little thank you to the snowflake that granted my wish.

A little magic…a little magic is everywhere!

THE END

Printed in Great Britain
by Amazon

50874171R00031